THE
COMPLETE
VEGETARIAN
RECIPES
COOKBOOK

TABLE OF CONTENTS

CHAPTER ONE

QUICK AND TASTY VEGETARIAN BREAKFAST RECIPES

Looking for quick, healthy and delicious on the go or leisurely breakfast options? We've got you covered with these fantastic bunch of delicious breakfast/brunch ideas that are fast, scrumptious and easy to make.

1. Tofu and Gorgonzola Scramble

Time: 20 Minutes

Ingredients:

- ¼ cup red onion (chopped)
- 2/3 cup white mushrooms (sliced)
- 4 tablespoons Gorgonzola cheese (crumbled /grated)
- 1 garlic clove (minced)
- 2 tablespoons olive oil
- 12-ounce firm tofu (cubed)
- 1 cup spinach

Method:

1. Heat skillet. Add olive oil.
2. Add onion, garlic, tofu until onion turns translucent.

3. Add mushrooms and cook until they turn soft for 5-7 minutes. Tofu should be slightly brownish.

4. Remove from heat. Combine spinach and cheese, and add to the tofu mixture until the Gorgonzola cheese melts and the spinach starts wilting.

2. Avocado and Goat Cheese Toast

Time: 10 Minutes

- Ingredients:
- 4 slices bread (crusty)
- ½ cup goat cheese (crumbled or grated)
- Red pepper flakes
- Extra virgin olive oil
- One ripe avocado
- Sea salt

Method:

1. Toast bread until it turns light brown and crunchy.
2. Mash avocado and divide equally into four parts.
3. Sprinkle grated goat cheese.
4. Add olive oil, followed by pepper flakes and salt.

3. Veggie Pita Pizza

Time: 25 minutes

Ingredients:

- 1 clove garlic (crushed, minced)
- ½ cup bell pepper (diced)
- ½ cup baby mushrooms (sliced)
- ½ cup red onion (diced)
- 1 cup spinach (roughly chopped)
- Hot sauce (as per taste)
- Black pepper (as per taste)
- 2 tablespoons Greek yogurt
- 1 ½ tablespoon sriracha sauce
- ½ cup cheese (shredded)
- Olive Oil for spraying
- Water (cooking)
- 1 pita bread (whole wheat)
- 1 egg (beaten)

Method:

1. Preheat oven to 180 degrees C. Add cooking spray on a medium sized .baking sheet.
2. Add little water to a skillet and heat until it turns very hot. Add garlic, mushrooms red onions, and pepper and keep cooking for 8 minutes or until mixture turns soft and mushy. Combine water as necessary.

3. Combine spinach and cook for a couple of minutes until it wilts.

4. Beat the egg, fiery sauce, and black pepper. Add to the vegetable mixture on the skillet and cook until the egg is completely scrambled on medium heat.

5. Bake the pita for 4-5 minutes until it turns golden brown.

6. Mix yogurt and sriracha, and combine well.

7. Spread yogurt and sriracha sauce on pita bread and add egg and veggie mixture.

8. Sprinkle cheese on top.

9. Cook for 4 minutes or until cheese goes gooey.

10. Cut into slices and serve.

4. Focaccia Tomato Basil Sandwiches

Time: 30 minutes

Ingredients (2 sandwiches)

- 1 yellow bell pepper (use roasted ones from the deli when you are short of time)
- 2 tbsps. sundried tomato puree
- 4 ripe halved ripe tomatoes
- One half of big focaccia bread
- 1 tbsp. olive oil
- 4 oz. (110 g) mozzarella sliced
- 8 basil leaves
- Ground pepper and table salt (as per taste)

Method:

1. Preheat broiler. Line pan with foil.
2. Grill peppers until blistered.
3. Wrap the pepper in foil to seal it and allow it to cool.
4. Cut the focaccia vertically half, and horizontally into quarters. Toast on both sides in the broiler.
5. Spread sun-dried tomato puree on both sides.
6. Line broiler with foil and place tomatoes on it. Drizzle with olive oil. Cook for 4-5 minutes until tomatoes have turned mushy. Sprinkle salt and pepper.
7. Cut pepper into strips and add pepper slices and tomatoes to the focaccia. Sprinkle mozzarella cheese and basil leaves. Drizzle oil from pan. Place the other half focaccia bread and serve warm.

5. Tasty Veggie Tacos

Time: 20-25 minutes (3 tacos)

Ingredients for filling

- 1 ½ garlic cloves (minced)
- Half zucchini (sliced into thin strips)
- Half red pepper (chopped)
- Half white onion (diced)
- ½ lime (juice)
- Salt, pepper flakes and black pepper ground (as per taste)
- 3 eggs (scrambled)
- 4-5 cherry tomatoes (chopped)
- 1 teaspoon olive oil
- 3 small to mid-sized tortillas
- Choice of garnishing – feta cheese, hot sauce, jalapeno, etc.

Method:

1. Heat skillet. When sufficiently heated, add olive oil.
2. Add onions and salt and cook until onions turn translucent for 5 minutes.
3. Introduce garlic and pepper flakes and sauté for 45 seconds to a minute.
4. Add zucchini and bell pepper until the mixture has gone soft for 5-7 minutes. We need a softened mixture not runny/mushy one.

5. Turn off heat and add lime juice. Add salt, stir well and set aside.

6. Scramble eggs and add hot sauce, black pepper, and salt. Cook on medium heat.

7. Fold in cherry tomatoes and set aside the mixture.

8. Warm tortilla on medium heat. Remove aside on a plate. Top it with eggs and veggie mixture. Garnish with feta, hot sauce, jalapeno, etc.

6. Tasty Tofu Burritos

Time: 15 minutes

Ingredients (2 burritos)

- 2 big mushrooms (sliced)
- 1 clove garlic (diced)
- ¼ cup red onion (diced)
- ½ package extra firm tofu (crumbled/grated)
- ¼ tsp of cumin, salt, pepper, turmeric, chili powder, garlic powder each mixed with 1 ½ tsp water.
- 2 wraps
- Lime juice 1tspn
- Lettuce (2 leaves)
- Sliced avocado (1 cup)
- Refried beans (1 cup)
- Salsa (as per taste)
- Cilantro leaves

Method:

1. Heat pan sufficiently
2. Introduce diced garlic, red pepper, mushrooms and onion and cook for about 10 minutes until the mixture turns soft and mushy.
3. Add tofu and the entire spices mixture into the pan.

4. Stir and cook until tofu is hot.

5. You can either heat refried beans separately or add them cold.

6. Add generous heaps of beans, cilantro, lettuce, avocado, lime juice and salsa to the wraps. Fill the tofu mixture.

7. Wrap and enjoy.

7. Fiery Baked Tomatoes and Eggs

Time: 25 minutes

Ingredients (serves 2)

- 2 tbsps. olive oil
- 1 red chili (deseed and chop finely)
- Coriander bunch small (chopped)
- 3 small red onions (chopped)
- 1 garlic clove
- 4 eggs
- 1 tsp castor sugar
- Cherry tomato cans (2 400 gm each)

Method:

1. Heat pan (with a lid). Slowly add oil. Add onions, garlic, chopped coriander and red chili for 5-10 minutes until the mixture softens. Combine tomatoes and castor sugar.

2. Allow the mixture to bubble for 10 minutes until it thickens.

3. The mixture can be frozen and stored for a month.

4. Use a large spoon to make four crevices in the sauce. Crack open an egg into each of the four openings. Cover and keep cooking on low to medium heat for 8-10 minutes until the eggs are done as per your preference.

5. Sprinkle some coriander leaves. Serve with warm crusty bread.

8. Pesto Toast

Time: 20 minutes

Ingredients: (2 toasts)

- ¼ cup hulled pumpkin seeds
- 1 medium clove garlic
- 1 big avocado
- Salt (as per taste)
- Basil leaves (1/3 cup)
- 1 tbsp. lemon juice

Optional accompaniments include cherry tomatoes, ground black pepper, and pepper flakes.

1. Add pumpkin seeds to a skillet and cook on slow to medium heat. Cook until the seeds crackle and make popping sounds. Remove from flame and set aside to cool.

2. Pit the avocados into two by scooping out its insides into a food processor. Add lemon juice, garlic, and salt as per taste. Blend until mixture turns smooth.

3. Add pumpkin seeds and basil to pulse the entire mixture until it is finely blended. Add more salt if necessary.

4. Toast bread, and spread a generous heap of avocado pesto on each slice. Serve with tomatoes. Top it with ground pepper and red pepper flakes. Serve hot.

9. Green Hummus (With Toast or Pita)

Time: 20 minutes

- Ingredients (Approx. 2 cups)
- ¼ cup tahini
- 2 tablespoons olive oil (keep more aside for drizzling on top)
- ½ cup fresh parsley (chopped)
- ¼ cup lemon juice
- ½ cup fresh tarragon (roughly chopped)
- Salt (as per taste)
- 1 garlic clove (chopped)
- One can of chickpeas (washed and drained)
- 3 tbsps. fresh chives (chopped)
- Fresh herbs for garnishing

Method:

1. Combine tahini and lemon juice into a creamy, smooth mixture. Whip it first before adding to a food processor.

2. Add olive oil, chives, garlic, tarragon, parsley and salt to the mixture and processes it again. Pause to scrape mixture from the bowl when necessary.

3. Add half the given quantity of chickpeas and process for a minute or two. Slowly add remainder chickpeas and process until mixture is smooth yet thick. Add water slowly if the mixture is too lumpy and process until you achieve the desired consistency.

4. Remove mixture in a bowl. Drizzle 1 teaspoon of olive oil.

5. Serve with pita bread or crusty bread or toast.

6. Refrigerate in a container and use as required until a week.

10. Savory Quinoa Bowl

Time: 15 minutes

Ingredients (single serving)

- 100 gm extra firm tofu (crumbled)
- ¼ cup cherry tomatoes
- 1 cup kale (tear into tiny pieces)
- ½ cup carrot (grated)
- ½ cup mushrooms (sliced)
- ½ teaspoon garlic powder
- ½ cup broccoli (chopped)
- ½ teaspoon curry powder (yellow)
- ½ teaspoon paprika
- ½ teaspoon onion powder
- Salt and pepper (as per taste)
- Half a lime
- ½ cup quinoa (cooked)
- ½ avocado (sliced)
- ½ cup sprouts (deli)

Method:

1. Heat a wok over high heat.
2. Combine spices and seasonings in a large bowl and keep aside.

3. When the wok is sufficiently heated, add mushrooms, carrot, and broccoli with a few drops of water. Cook for about 6-7 minutes until vegetables turn mushy.

4. Reduce heat and combine cherry tomatoes, spice mixture, and kale. Continue to stir and cook until the kale wilts. Keep splashing water to prevent the mixture from sticking, burning or overcooking.

5. Add lime juice and tofu until it scrambles into the mixture and turns golden brown.

6. Add the mixture to a quinoa bowl.

7. Sprinkle the entire mixture with sprouts and/or sliced avocado. Add more lime, salt, and pepper if required.

11. Chickpea Omelet

Time: 15 Minutes

Ingredients (for 3 small sized omelets)

- 1 cup chickpea flour
- ½ teaspoon each of onion, garlic, white pepper and black pepper powder
- 1/3 cup yeast
- ½ teaspoon baking soda
- 4 ounces mushrooms (sautéed)
- 3 green onions (chopped)

Method:

1. Mix chickpea flour, garlic powder, onion powder, black pepper and white pepper, yeast and baking soda in a bowl. Add some water to make a smooth batter.

2. Heat pan sufficiently. Pour batter into the pan and spread evenly. Add a couple of tablespoons of mushrooms and green onions for cooking each omelet. Keep flipping it periodically until both sides are cooked evenly.

3. Top your omelet with spinach, hot sauce, salsa, tomatoes and any other topping of your choice.

CHAPTER TWO

QUICK AND EASY VEGETARIAN LUNCH RECIPES

1. Egg Fried Cauliflower

Ingredients (2 servings)

- 2 tbsps. coconut oil
- Slices of yellow, red and green (diced)
- A small onion (diced)
- Cherry tomatoes (half punnet)
- 1 full head cauliflower (grated). To save time, you can use premade Tesco ones
- ½ Peas (fresh or frozen)
- 2 beaten eggs
- Salt and black pepper (as per taste)
- Optional - Soya sauce (use tamari soya sauce if you are looking for a gluten-free alternative)

Method:

1. Heat oil in a large wok. Add onion and peppers and cook for 2-3 minutes.
2. Add tomatoes and peas. Fry this mixture for another 3 minutes.

3. Combine beaten eggs with the vegetables and spread evenly, so the vegetable mixture is completely covered. Spread evenly instead of stirring. Wait for a minute before mixing the eggs to form a scrambled preparation.

4. Add cauliflower and sauté for another 5-7 minutes till the mixture turns soft.

5. Season with soya sauce, salt, and pepper.

Tip – This mixture can make for scrumptious wrap fillings or can be eaten by itself as a quick, easy and delicious lunch option.

2. Greek Nachos

Time: 20 Minutes

Ingredients (3 servings)

- ½ tablespoon lemon juice
- Fresh ground pepper (as per taste)
- ½ cup lettuce (chopped)
- 1 ½ cups whole grain pita chips
- ¼ cup grape tomatoes (quartered)
- ¼ cup feta cheese (crumbled)
- 1 tablespoon olives (Kalamata chopped)
- 1 tablespoon red onion (chopped)
- ½ cup hummus
- ½ tablespoon oregano for seasoning
- 1 tbsp. olive oil

Method

1. Mix hummus (leave some aside), olive oil, pepper and lemon juice.
2. Arrange a layer of pita on a plate. Dollop hummus on the chips.
3. Add lettuce, feta cheese, olives, red onions, and tomatoes. Add a dollop of the hummus mixture set aside in a bowl. Top off with oregano.

3. Delicious Thai Noodle Soup

Ingredients (2 bowls)

- ½ packet or 4-ounce rice vermicelli noodles
- ½ freshly peeled and crushed ginger
- 1 ½ cups vegetable stock (without salt)
- ½ cup carrots (thinly sliced)
- ½ red pepper (thinly sliced)
- 2 garlic cloves (crushed)
- Half cucumber (thinly sliced lengthwise)
- 2 ½ tablespoons fresh herbs (mixed)
- 3 tablespoons roasted peanuts without salt
- 1 teaspoon chili oil
- 1 ½ low sodium soy sauce

Method:

1. Cook noodles as mentioned on the packet and drain.

2. Heat pan sufficiently. Slowly add oil. Throw in ginger and garlic to cook for about 1-2 minutes, continuously stirring the mixture.

3. Introduce stock and low sodium soy sauce. Let it boil while stirring continuously.

4. Simmer mixture for 10-12 minutes.

5. Add cucumber, carrots, and pepper in a bowl and combine nicely. Portion out noodles into two serving bowls.

6. Top each bowl with half the vegetable mixture.

7. Pour half of the stock into each bowl.

8. Sprinkle with peanuts and herbs.

9. Drizzle with some chili oil for added flavor.

4. Nuts Fried Rice

Ingredients (3 servings)

- 1 ½ tablespoons sesame oil
- 1 ½ cups broccoli florets
- 1 package pre-made brown rice
- 4 ounces sliced shiitake mushrooms
- ½ cup roasted cashews (not salted)
- 1 beaten egg
- 1 ½ tablespoon low sodium soy sauce
- ¼ cup peanut butter
- ¼ teaspoons black pepper
- ½ tablespoon rice vinegar
- ½ tablespoon water
- ½ tablespoon sesame seeds (toasted)

Method:

1. Heat ½ tablespoon oil on a high flame in a large nonstick skillet.

2. Add mushrooms and broccoli. Continue cooking for 5-7 more minutes. Turn off heat and set aside.

3. Add rest of the 1 tablespoon of oil. Introduce rice along with nuts. Cook for another 7-8 minutes.

4. Combine eggs to cook for a couple of minutes until they are well cooked.

5. Add broccoli, half a tablespoon of soy sauce and pepper.

6. Add remaining 1 ½ tablespoon soy sauce, vinegar, peanut butter, and half a tablespoon of water in a bowl. Top rice with peanut butter mix and sprinkle sesame seeds for extra taste.

5. Delicious Panzanella Salad (Light Bread and Tomatoes Italian Salad)

Time: 20 minutes

Ingredients (one large bowl)

- 3 tbsps. olive oil
- 2 large tomatoes (ripe and cubed)
- 1 yellow pepper (cubed)
- 15 basil leaves (chopped)
- 1 cucumber (sliced into ½ inch slices)
- ½ red onion (sliced thinly)

Dressing:

- 1 tsp garlic (crushed)
- 1/2 cup oil olive
- ½ tsp Dijon mustard
- 3 1/2 tbsps. capers
- ¼ tsp fresh ground black pepper
- Salt (as per taste)
- 3 ½ tbsps. wine vinegar

Method:

1. Make the dressing by combining garlic, vinegar, olive oil (half quantity), mustard, salt, and pepper.
2. Add rest of the olive oil to a pan. Cook bread cubes on low heat for 8-10 minutes until they turn golden brown.
3. Add more olive oil as required.

4. Mix cucumber, bell pepper, red onion, tomato, capers and basil in a big bowl.

5. Add the vinaigrette along with cooked bread cubes to it and toss.

6. Combine seasoning (salt and pepper)

6. Baba Ghanoush

Time: 15 minutes

Ingredients (2 bowls)

- 4 small aubergines
- Salt and pepper (as per taste)
- garlic cloves (chopped roughly)
- 3 tbsps. parsley (chopped)
- 2 pinches red chili powder
- 4 tbsps. tahini paste
- 40 ml lemon juice
- 2 tbsps. olive oil (optional for drizzle)

Method:

1. Peel aubergines and add its flesh to a processor along with other ingredients.
2. Blend until you get a smooth mixture.
3. Season with salt, pepper, chili powder, parsley and olive oil (optional).
4. Enjoy with pita bread.

7. Easy Veggie Muffins

Time: 20 minutes

Ingredients (4 servings)

- 4 Muffins (Toasted English ones)
- 1 cup alfalfa sprouts
- 1 small onion (chopped)
- 1 avocado (mashed)
- 1 tomato (chopped)
- 5 tbsps. salad dressing (ranch style)
- 1 cup cheddar cheese (smoked)
- 5 tbsps. well toasted black sesame seeds

Method:

1. Begin by preheating oven on the broil mode.
2. Put a muffin on the cookie sheet open after splitting.
3. Spread every half with avocado by portioning all ingredients evenly. Cover every half with tomatoes, cheese, onion, sprouts, dressing and sesame seeds.
4. Broil until cheese melts into a golden brown and bubbles.

8. Light and Delicious Pasta Salad

Time: 20 minutes

Ingredients (serves 4-6)

Method:

- 1/2 box tri-colored pasta
- 1 ½ cup red onions (chopped)
- 1/2 lb. sliced cottage cheese
- ½ lb. provolone cheese (cubed)
- 1 ½ cup green pepper
- ½ cup black olives (sliced)
- 1 cup tomatoes (diced)

Dressing

- ¾ cup extra virgin olive oil
- 1 tablespoon oregano
- ¾ cup wine vinegar
- Salt and pepper
- ¾ cup sugar

Method:

1. Combine all salad dressing ingredients and keep it aside.
2. Prepare pasta as per box instructions.
3. Add cottage cheese slices.

4. Mix cottage cheese, chopped ingredients with cooked pasta.

5. Add dressing and chill for a while if you want a cold salad. If you like a more moist salad texture, pour additional olive oil or vinegar.

6. Top with cheese before serving.

9. Mexican Guacamole with Tortilla

Time: 20 minutes

Ingredients (2-3 servings)

- 2 ½ Roma tomatoes (diced)
- 3 avocados (peeled and mashed)
- ½ cup onion (finely chopped)
- 1 tsp garlic (minced)
- 3 tbsps. fresh cilantro (chopped)
- 1/2 lime juice

Method:

1. Combine lime juice, salt, pepper and mashed avocados.
2. Add onion, cilantro, garlic, and onion.
3. Add more pepper if required.
4. Refrigerate to serve cold or serve immediately
5. The versatile guacamole can eaten by itself as a salad or combined with tortillas or even as a wrap filling for quick, easy and delicious lunches.

10. Parmesan Spinach Baked Rice

Time: 30 minutes

Ingredients (2 servings)

- 1 package frozen spinach (chopped). Ensure excess water is removed from it.

- 2 ½ cups cooked rice

- 2 cups cheese (grated)

- 1 cup parmesan cheese (crumbled)

- 1/2 cup butter

- 2 big green onions (chopped)

- 1 garlic clove (minced)

- ¾ cup milk

- 3 big eggs (beaten)

- Salt and pepper (as per taste)

- ¼ cup parmesan for garnishing

- Mozzarella grated (optional garnish)

Method:

1. Preheat oven to 180 degrees C and lightly drizzle medium-sized baking dish.

2. Combine butter, cheddar cheese, rice, onions, eggs, milk, parmesan cheese, spinach and garlic until it is fully combined.

3. Add salt and pepper as per taste.

4. Place the mixture on the baking dish and garnish with parmesan.

5. Bake for 20 minutes. If you're garnishing with mozzarella, add it during the last 3-4 minutes of the baking time.

11. Mexican Pico De Gallo

Time: 15 Minutes

Ingredients (2 servings)

- 2-3 Jalapeno peppers (sliced)
- ½ tbsp. lime juice
- 4 fully ripe plum tomatoes (roughly chopped)
- 1 white onion (diced)
- Salt (as per taste)
- 1 cup coriander (roughly chopped)

Method:

1. Mix all ingredients and cover.
2. Refrigerate if you want to enjoy it cold. Otherwise, it is good to go as it is. Avoid storing it and consume on the same day for freshness.

12. Super Vegetarian Club Sandwich

Time: 10 minutes

Ingredients (serves 1)

- 3 slices large granary bread
- Lemon juice (one squeeze)
- 1 carrot (peel and grate coarsely)
- 2 tomatoes (sliced thickly)
- 1 tbsp. olive oil
- 2 tbsps. hummus
- 1 handful of watercress

Method:

1. Toast bread lightly. In the meantime, mix carrot, lemon juice, olive oil, and watercress.
2. Spread hummus on each toast slice.
3. Add watercress and carrot mixture to one slice. Put another slice on top of it and top it with a thick tomato slice. Finally, add the third slice (hummus side will be down).
4. Cut sandwich into quarters and enjoy.

13. Tomato Mozzie Burger

Time: 10 Minutes

Ingredients (serves 3)

- 3 large ripened tomatoes
- Salt and pepper (as per taste)
- 4 ounces mozzarella (unsalted)
- 1 tbsp. olive oil
- ½ large garlic clove (sliced thinly)
- 1 sprig fresh basil leaves

Method:

1. Heat oven at 450 degrees F. Cut the tomato into two horizontal halves. You may have to cut the bottom of the tomato to make it stand properly.

2. Arrange tomatoes with the cut portion up on a foil-lined baking sheet (rimmed) or roasting pan.

3. Cover with oil. Add seasoning as required. Sprinkle thinly sliced garlic over tomatoes.

4. Roast until it is softened for around 12-15 minutes.

5. In the meantime, cut mozzarella into three ½ inch slices. Use a spatula to sandwich the slice between two warm tomato halves until the heat slightly melts the mozzarella.

6. Drizzle tomatoes with all the accumulated juices in the pan and garnish with fresh basil before serving.

14. Israeli Salad

Time- 15 Minutes

Ingredients (4 servings)

- 1/2 lb. cucumbers (Persian or other variants diced)
- 1/3 cup onion (chopped, minced)
- ½ lb. fresh fully ripe tomatoes (sliced)
- ½ cup fresh parsley (minced)
- Sal (as per taste)
- 1 ½ tbsps. extra virgin oil olive
- 1 ½ fresh lemon juice

Method:

1. Combine diced cucumbers with all ingredients.
2. Combine well until the veggies combine with oil, fresh parsley, salt and lemon juice.
3. Tastes best at room temperature, though you can refrigerate if you prefer a more chilled version. Enjoy as a salad or a healthy, light lunch.

CHAPTER 3

SIMPLE AND DELICIOUS VEGETARIAN DINNERS

1. African Sweet Potatoes in Peanut Soup

Time: 25 minutes

Ingredients (2-3 servings)

- ½ tsp peanut oil
- 1 ½ garlic clove (crushed)
- 2 c low sodium vegetable broth
- ¼ can tomatoes (diced)
- ½ onion (finely chopped)
- 1-inch ginger (finely chopped)
- 1 lb. sweet potatoes (peel and cut into one-inch chunky pieces)
- ½ c peanut butter
- ½ tbsp. tomato paste
- ½ tsp cayenne (depending on taste you can add or reduce quantity)
- 1 c collard greens
- Salt as per taste
- Toasted peanuts for garnish

Method:

1. Heat peanut oil in soup pot. Add garlic, ginger, sweet potatoes and onion. Cook on medium flame until the mixture softens.

2. Add tomatoes, cayenne, tomato paste, peanut butter, and broth. Keep stirring to mix ingredients well until it begins to simmer.

3. Simmer on low heat for 8-10 minutes by covering the pot.

4. Coarsely mash the potatoes with a masher.

5. Add greens and simmer without covering the pot for 3-4 minutes.

6. Add salt as per taste.

7. Serve on a bed of brown taste.

8. Garnish with toasted peanuts.

2. Dutch Mosterdsoep Soup

Time: 20 minutes

Ingredients (2-3 servings)

- 3 cups vegetable stock
- ½ cup flour
- 3 tbsps. mustard
- ¼ cup butter
- 1 tbsps. whipped cream
- Salt and pepper (as per taste)

Method:

1. Add vegetable stock to pan. Bring to boil while stirring.
2. In another pan, melt butter and add flour. Keep stirring to avoid formations of lumps. Cook until you get a smooth mixture and for about 4-5 minutes.
3. Add stock gradually at about 1/4th cup each time. Stir continuously. Cook continuously till mixture has an even and creamy consistency, without lumps.
4. Simmer on low heat after adding entire stock for 12 minutes.
5. Add whipped cream on top and serve hot.

3. Rice and Tofu Filled Peppers (a delicious vegetarian twist on a classic beef recipe)

Time: 30 minutes

Ingredients (4 portions)

- 2 cups cooked brown or white rice

- 2 ½ cups marinara sauce

- 1 garlic clove (finely chopped)

- 3 tbsps. olive oil

- 2 red bell peppers (cut into halves)

- 4 slices of tomato

- 2 cups mozzarella cheese (shredded)

- 1 packet of extra firm tofu (diced after draining)

- 2 yellow bell peppers (cut into halves)

- Salt and pepper

Method:

1. Heat oil in a skillet and cook on low heat. Introduce tofu and finely chopped garlic and keep cooking for around 5-6 minutes.

2. Mix a 1 cup of marinara sauce.

3. Add salt and pepper as per taste and cook until mixture turns golden brown.

4. Preheat oven to 175 degrees c.

5. Add equal portions of rice into each of the peppers. Add remaining marinara sauce and a cup of cheese.

6. Add tofu, again equally portioned into 4 peppers.

7. Place sliced tomato on each pepper and garnish with the remaining cup of cheese.

8. Bake peppers for 20 minutes till the cheese melts. Serve hot.

4. Thai Peanut Vegetarian Pasta

Time: 25 Minutes

Ingredients (2 servings)

- 1 red onion (thin half circular slices)
- ½ large carrot (cut into thin sticks)
- ½ tbsp. grated ginger
- 1 clove garlic
- 8 ounces cremini mushrooms (sliced)
- 1 tbsp. olive oil
- ½ large bell pepper (sliced)
- 3 tbsps. soy sauce
- 1 tbsp. peanut butter
- 4 ounces whole wheat spaghetti
- ½ lime juice
- ¼ cilantro (chopped)
- ¼ peanuts (chopped)
- 1 ½ tbsps. rice vinegar

Method:

1. Heat olive oil in a skillet on low flame. Introduce onion, carrots, and mushrooms. Cook continuously for 7 minutes or until the mixture turns soft. Add ginger, garlic, and pepper. Sauté for 2-3 minutes.

2. Mix soya sauce, peanut butter, and rice vinegar. Add this mixture to the skillet. Pour in the broth slowly. Stir and mix.

3. Add spaghetti and cook until it softens. Increase heat, cover skillet and bring to boil.

4. Remove cover and lower heat. Cook for 9-10 minutes or until the pasta gets semi cooked or al Dante. It should absorb the liquid. Keep stirring.

5. Garnish with cilantro, lime juice, and chopped peanuts.

5. Spicy Vegetarian Tikka Masala

Time: 25 minutes

Ingredients (5 servings)

- 1 tsp turmeric (ground)
- ¼ tsp red pepper (crushed)
- 2 packages 14 ounces each of extra firm tofu
- 2 tbsps. canola oil
- 1 ½ large bell pepper (sliced)
- 1 tbsp. ginger (minced)
- 1 ½ large onion (sliced)
- 28-ounce can of sundried tomatoes
- 1 tbsp. flour
- 2 garlic cloves (crushed)

Method:

1. Mix garam masala, salt, turmeric and red pepper (can be skipped if you want to avoid extra spice in a bowl.

2. Add one inch cubed tofu pieces in a bowl with a tablespoon of spice mix.

3. Heat 1 tablespoon oil on low flame. Throw in tofu. Keep cooking it for 10-12 minutes, stirring occasionally until tofu turns golden brown. Transfer mix on plate.

4. Add remaining oil, onion, ginger, garlic, bell pepper and keep cooking the mixture, until it gets browned in 5 minutes.

5. Add flour along with remaining spice mix. Let it coated with the spice mix for a couple of minutes.

6. Combine tomatoes and cook on low heat for 5-6 minutes (stirring often) until vegetables have softened.

7. Add tofu back into the pan, cook while stirring occasionally for 3-4 minutes. Remove from flame. Stir half and half.

8. Enjoy with a side of brown rice.

6. Chili Veg Macaroni and Cheese

Time: 20 minutes

Ingredients (3 servings)
- 500 ml tomato soup
- 1 ½ medium onion (finely chopped)
- 1/ tsp paprika (smoked)
- ½ tsp red chili powder (adjust as per taste)
- ¼ tsp ground cumin
- 5 midsized mushrooms (sliced)
- 120 g cooked kidney beans
- Salt and pepper (as per taste)
- 1 bell pepper (sliced)
- 180 gm pasta (uncooked)
- ½ cup water
- 80 gm cheddar cheese (grated)
- Fresh spring onion and cilantro (chopped)

Method:
1. If you are using frozen soup, defrost in microwave for 12 minutes.
2. In the meantime, heat oil in a pan. Add peppers, onions, chili and finally, mushrooms.
3. Cook on low heat for a few minutes until the vegetables achieve a soft texture.
4. Add kidney beans and all spices. Season it well.

5. Add tomato soup, uncooked pasta along with water. Combine to simmer for 15-20 minutes. Stir regularly until pasta is nicely cooked. Add some more water if required.

6. Once ready, add half of the cheddar cheese to the pasta and combine. Top the pasta with remaining cheese and cook on low heat until the cheese melts into a golden brown.

7. Garnish with fresh cilantro, coriander, and spring onions. Serve hot with garlic bread or an accompaniment of your choice.

7. Chickpea Shakshuka

Time: 30 minutes

Ingredients (4-6 servings)
- 2 tbsp. olive oil
- ½ red bell pepper (chopped)
- ½ cup white onion (diced)
- 1 28-ounce can tomato puree
- 1 tbsp. maple syrup
- 1 ½ tsp smoked paprika
- 4 garlic cloves (chopped)
- 2 tsp ground cumin
- 3 tbsps. tomato paste
- 2 tsp chili powder
- ¼ tsp cinnamon (ground)
- 2 cups chickpeas (cooked and drained)
- Lemon slices
- Salt (as per taste)

Method:
1. Heat a big rimmed skillet over reduced/low heat. Slowly introduce olive oil, onion, garlic and bell pepper. Cook mixture for around 5-7 minutes, while stirring regularly. The mixture should be soft and aromatic.
2. Add tomato paste, maple syrup, tomato puree, salt, cumin, paprika, cinnamon powder, and cardamom. Mix well.

3. Simmer on low flame for 3-4 minutes stirring the mixture regularly. If you prefer a smoother and creamier texture, you may want to use a blender. However, you can leave it as it is if you prefer a more coarse result.

4. Add chickpeas and olives and stir the mixture to combine all ingredients well. Allow the flavors to blend, while simmering mixture for 15 minutes.

5. Adjust seasonings as required. For more smokiness, you can add more paprika. Similarly, if you want it sweeter, add more maple syrup.

6. Garnish with lemon juice, more olives and chopped greens (optional parsley or cilantro).

7. Serve with pasta, rice or bread. It can stay in the refrigerator for a maximum of 4 days, and frozen for a maximum of one month.

8. Black Bean Burger

Time: 25 Minutes

Ingredients (4 burger patties)

- 1 slice toasted and torn bread
- 1 ½ tsp fresh lime juice
- ½ tsp grated lime (rind)
- ½ walnut (chopped)
- 1/2 cup onion (chopped
- ¾ tsp cumin (ground)
- 1 can of unsalted black beans (wash and drain)
- ½ tsp hot sauce
- 1 ½ tbsps. garlic (chopped)
- 4 tsp olive oil
- 1 egg (beaten)
- Salt (as per taste)

Method:

1. Pulse bread in food processor 4-5 times before transferring to a large bowl.
2. Add onion, lime juice, salt, rind, beans, and garlic in processor. Pulse about 4-5 times.
3. Add bean mix, hot sauce, egg and walnut to the breadcrumbs.
4. Separate the mixture into equal parts and shape each one into a thick (3/4th inch) patty.

5. Heat oil in a pan and add patties. Cook evenly on slow heat for 7-8 minutes on each side until they achieve a brownish tinge.

6. Add sauces of your choice along with a slice of tomato and other raw veggies in burger buns to enjoy as delicious vegetarian burgers.

9. Potato - Mushroom Curry

Time: 20 Minutes

Ingredients (serves 4)

- 1 onion (chopped roughly)
- 1 big potato
- 1 large aubergine (chopped into tiny chunky pieces)
- 2 tbsps. oil
- 300 gm button mushrooms
- 200 ml vegetable stock
- 3-4 tbsps. curry paste
- Coriander (chopped)
- Salt
- 350 ml coconut milk

Method:

1. Add oil heating pan sufficiently. Introduce potato and roughly chopped onion. Cook covered for 5-10 minutes till your potatoes have softened.

2. Add mushrooms and chunks of aubergine and cook for 3-4 minutes.

3. Combine curry paste, coconut milk, and vegetable stock.

4. Boil mixture followed by simmering it on low heat for 10-12 minutes or till the potatoes get a soft texture.

5. Garnish with coriander and serve with rice, bread or naan.

10. Thai Red Vegetable Curry

Time: 25 Minutes

Ingredients (4 servings)

- 3 tbsps. olive oil
- 3 cloves garlic (minced)
- 1 large red bell pepper (sliced into strips)
- 1 tbsp. ginger (grated finely)
- 1 large yellow bell pepper (sliced into strips)
- 1 medium sized onion (chopped)
- Salt
- 1 ½ can coconut milk
- 3 carrots (peeled, sliced into ½ inch thick round pieces
- 2 tbsps. soy sauce
- 2 cups kale (thinly sliced)
- ½ cup water
- 2 tsp brown sugar
- 3 tbsps. Thai red curry paste
- Fresh basil or cilantro(chopped)
- Red pepper flakes (optional garnish)
- 3 tsp rice vinegar
- Sriracha/chili garlic sauce

Method:

1. Heat a large skillet. Introduce oil. Add onion and salt to cook until onion goes soft for 5-7 minutes. Keep stirring frequently.

2. Add garlic followed by ginger and cook for 2-3 minutes, while stirring continuously.

3. Add carrots and peppers and cook until peppers are slightly soft for 5 minutes while stirring continuously. Combine flavorsome curry paste and mix nicely for 2-3 minutes.

4. Add coconut milk, kale, sugar, and water. Mix well. Simmer on slow heat. Cook until bell peppers and carrots become soft for 7-10 minutes. Stir frequently.

5. Remove from pot and season with vinegar, tamari or optional garnishing. Adjust salt as per taste.

6. Serve with a bed of rice.

Printed in Great Britain
by Amazon